Careers without College

Customer Service Representative

by Kathryn A. Quinlan

Consultant:

Margery Steinberg, Ph.D.
Associate Professor of Marketing
University of Hartford

CAPSTONE
HIGH/LOW BOOKS
an imprint of Capstone Press
Mankato, Minnesota

Capstone High/Low Books are published by Capstone Press
818 North Willow Street, Mankato, Minnesota 56001
http://www.capstone-press.com

Library of Congress Cataloging-in-Publication Data
Quinlan, Kathryn A.
    Customer service representative/by Kathryn A. Quinlan.
    p. cm. — (Careers without college)
    Includes bibliographical references (p. 45) and index.
    Summary: Introduces the position of customer service representative, including
educational requirements, training, duties, salary, employment outlook, and possible
future positions.
    ISBN 0-7368-0174-X
    1. Customer services—Vocational guidance—Juvenile literature. [1. Customer
services—Vocational guidance. 2. Vocational guidance.] I. Title. II. Series: Careers
without college (Mankato, Minn.)
HF5415.5.Q557 1999
658.8'12'02373—dc21   98-31593
                                                                            CIP
                                                                            AC

Editorial Credits
Karen L. Daas, editor; Steve Christensen, cover designer;
    Kimberly Danger and Sheri Gosewisch, photo researchers

Photo Credits
International Stock/Hal Kern, 44
Jerry Ruff, 6, 20, 30, 37
Leslie O'Shaughnessy, 38
PhotoBank, Inc., 24; PhotoBank, Inc./David R. Frazier, 8; Pat Harrison, 23;
    Gary Conner, 27; Bill Lai, 41
Photo Network, 34; Photo Network/Myrleen Cate, 4
Photophile, cover
Shaffer Photography/James L. Shaffer, 14, 29
The Picture Cube/John Coletti, 10; Rick Scott 18
Unicorn Stock Photos/Jeff Greenberg, 32
Uniphoto, 16; Uniphoto/Melanie Carr, 12

Table of Contents

Fast Facts

Career Title——————————Customer service representative

Minimum Educational————U.S.: high school diploma
Requirement   Canada: high school diploma

Certification Requirement———U.S.: none
Canada: none

Salary Range——————————U.S.: $9,568 to $32,812
(U.S. Bureau of Labor Statistics and   Canada: $16,500 to $45,300
Human Resources Development
Canada, late 1990s figures)   (Canadian dollars)

Job Outlook——————————U.S.: faster than average growth
(U.S. Bureau of Labor Statistics and   Canada: fair
Human Resources Development
Canada, late 1990s projections)

DOT Clusters —————————Professional, technical, and
(Dictionary of Occupational Titles)   managerial occupations;
clerical occupations

DOT Numbers——————————305.362-026, 239.362-014

GOE Number——————————None available
(Guide for Occupational Exploration)

NOC————————————————145
(National Occupational Classification—Canada)

5

Chapter 1

Job Responsibilities

Many companies have customer service representatives. These representatives help customers. Customers are people who buy or use a company's products or services.

Customer service representatives usually are the first people to speak to a company's customers. They answer customers' questions. Representatives offer information about a company's products or services. They sometimes take orders and collect information from customers. Representatives help solve customers' problems.

Customer service representatives answer questions.

Order Representatives

Some customer service representatives work for catalog companies. These companies mail magazines that list their products to customers. The customers then contact companies to place their orders. Customers may contact companies by mail, phone, or over the Internet.

Catalog company representatives often talk to customers on the phone. These representatives answer customers' questions about products. They also may help customers place orders.

Customer service representatives record information about customers' orders. They record what customers order. They also record customers' names, addresses, and telephone numbers. Representatives usually enter this information into computers.

Customers call companies when they have questions about their orders. Representatives handle these calls. They may need to check up on customers' orders.

Catalog company representatives often talk to customers on the phone.

ervice Desk
changes & Refunds
ecks Accepted at Any Register
y Refunded Within 30 Days with Register Receipt
2
CLOSED
GAGE
your protection,
swimwear
not returnable

Retail Representatives

Some customer service representatives work for stores. These retail representatives answer customers' questions about a store's products. They may explain product warranties to customers. Many manufacturers and sellers offer these guarantees. Most companies fix or replace broken products for free if the products have warranties.

Retail representatives also may help customers order products. Sometimes stores do not have the products customers want. Then retail representatives order these products. For example, retail representatives at music stores may order compact discs for customers.

Information Representatives

Some customer service representatives are information representatives. These representatives provide information to customers. Information representatives

Some customer service representatives help customers in stores.

Some information representatives work in hotels.

work for businesses such as hotels, motels, airlines, and travel agencies.

Hotel and motel information representatives help customers both over the telephone and in person. Some customers call to reserve rooms. Representatives record customers' names and the dates of their planned visits. They tell customers about hotel rates. They may offer information about nearby restaurants or places to visit. Representatives listen to any concerns customers may have about their rooms. They try to make sure customers are comfortable.

Information representatives also work for travel businesses. For example, airlines hire representatives to help customers reserve seats on airplanes. These representatives also answer questions about flight times and other customer concerns. Representatives at travel agencies help customers plan trips. They may offer information about places to visit. They also may reserve seats on airplanes for customers. These representatives may reserve hotel rooms for customers.

Chapter 2

What the Job Is Like

Customer service representatives experience both the benefits and challenges of working with people. They help many polite people. But they sometimes must help people who are upset because their expectations were not met. Customer service representatives must remain polite and calm at all times.

Customer service representatives often help many customers during a day. This customer contact helps representatives understand their customers' needs. Representatives then can offer

Customer service representatives help many customers every day.

their customers better service. They also have the opportunity to improve customers' opinions of their companies.

Challenges on the Job

Skillful customer service representatives are pleasant with all customers. Most customers are friendly when representatives are polite.

Customer service representatives' jobs can be stressful. For example, many companies require representatives to answer a certain number of calls each hour. But representatives cannot hurry through calls. They must take the time to listen to customers, answer questions, and help with problems. This can put pressure on representatives.

Customer service representatives often answer the same questions many times a day. Many customers have similar problems and questions. Customer service representatives must remain patient and helpful with each customer.

Skillful customer service representatives are pleasant with all customers.

Many customer service representatives work in call centers.

Call Centers

Many customer service representatives work in call centers. Representatives who work in call centers talk to customers on the phone. These representatives usually do not meet with customers.

Most customer service representatives in call centers do not have their own offices. They share a large work area with other representatives. They have their own workstations in this area. Workstations usually include a desk, telephone, and computer. Customer service representatives spend most of the day at their workstations. They need to be available to answer customers' calls.

Many utility companies have call centers. Utility companies include gas, water, telephone, and electricity companies. Customers call utility companies to set up utility service. They call if they have questions about their utility bills. Customers also call if they need to change their service. Customer service representatives answer these calls. They also schedule repairs for people who are having problems with their service.

Offices

Some customer service representatives work with customers in person. These representatives also may talk to customers on the phone. But they usually do not answer as many calls as representatives who work in call centers.

Customer service representatives at banks often meet with customers. These representatives may help customers open new accounts. They answer customers' questions about different kinds of accounts. Representatives enter customers' account information into computers. They make sure this information is correct.

Stores

Customer service representatives sometimes work in stores. These retail representatives usually work at customer service counters. They answer customers' questions. Retail representatives may help customers return products that do not fit their needs.

Retail representatives may help customers with special purchases. For example, they often help customers buy gift certificates. These documents can be used to buy products at the store. Customers often buy certificates as gifts for other people.

Some representatives work at customer service counters in stores.

Hours

Full-time customer service representatives usually work 40 hours each week. Some customer service representatives work during the day. But many companies provide service 24 hours a day. This means some representatives must work at night and on weekends.

Customer service representatives may need to work more than 40 hours a week. For example, representatives who work in stores may work more hours during busy seasons.

Personal Qualities

Customer service representatives must be polite, patient, and friendly. They represent their companies to the public. Representatives talk to many types of people every day. They need to explain their companies' products or services clearly. They also must listen carefully to their customers' needs.

Representatives must be honest, trustworthy, and accurate. They need to provide correct

Customer service representatives may explain a company's products or services to customers.

information to customers. They should not guess if they cannot answer customers' questions. Representatives who provide incorrect information can cause their companies to lose customers.

Chapter 3

Training

People usually do not need formal training or a college degree to become a customer service representative. Most representatives in the United States and Canada have high school diplomas. Customer service representatives usually receive training on the job. They learn about their companies' products or services as they work.

Scripts

Many companies have prepared scripts that customer service representatives follow during telephone calls. This written information guides representatives through calls. Scripts provide information about companies. Many scripts

High school students can prepare to be customer service representatives.

include answers to questions that customers often ask. Representatives usually practice scripts with other representatives before they answer phone calls. This helps them become more comfortable with the scripts.

Managers sometimes listen to customer service representatives' calls. Managers listen to make sure representatives know about companies' products and services. They also make sure representatives are polite and helpful to customers. Managers may give advice to representatives. This helps representatives improve their service skills.

Training Sessions

Customer service representatives often attend training sessions. They learn about companies' products and services. They practice answering questions that customers often ask. Representatives also learn how to speak with customers. They learn how to deal with customers in many situations.

New representatives also train with experienced representatives. New representatives may watch

Students who want to become customer service representatives can improve their writing skills.

experienced representatives with customers. Then new representatives help customers. They may need to ask experienced representatives questions as they work.

Skills
Customer service representatives need good computer skills. Representatives must learn to use companies' computer programs to locate and save customers' information. They also need to enter information into computers quickly and correctly.

Customer service representatives must think and react quickly. They must be able to answer questions about the products and services companies offer.

Representatives must have excellent communication skills. They must understand what information customers need. They must be able to help customers solve problems.

What Students Can Do Now
Students can take several classes to prepare to be customer service representatives. Students who

Customer service representatives use computers to find and save customers' information.

want to enter this field should take communications classes. These classes help students improve their speaking, listening, and writing skills.

Computer classes also are helpful for students who want to be customer service representatives. These classes help students learn basic computer

programs. Students can improve their keyboarding skills in these classes.

Part-time jobs can help students prepare to be customer service representatives. For example, students can work as retail salespeople. These people assist customers who buy products. Students also can work as cashiers. Cashiers use cash registers to add up customers' purchases or bills. They collect customers' money and give them change. All of these jobs give students experience in working with people.

Volunteer positions also can help students prepare to be customer service representatives. Volunteers offer to do a job without pay. Students can volunteer at community centers, hospitals, and schools. They may answer phones and provide information. They also gain experience in working with all types of people.

Part-time jobs can help students prepare to be customer service representatives.

Chapter 4

Salary and Job Outlook

Salaries for customer service representatives vary greatly. In the United States, information representatives earn between $11,076 and $29,952 per year (all figures late 1990s). Information representatives work at hotels, airports, and banks.

Order representatives in the United States earn between $9,568 and $32,812. These customer service representatives take customers' orders. Many order representatives work for catalog companies.

Some information representatives work in the travel business.

Retail representatives in the United States earn between $13,780 and $30,826. These customer service representatives work for stores.

Customer service representatives in Canada earn between $16,500 and $45,300 per year. Most representatives in Canada are retail representatives. The average salary for these representatives is about $35,700.

Benefits

Most full-time customer service representatives receive benefits. Benefits are payments or services in addition to a salary or wage. For example, many employers offer health insurance. Health insurance helps people pay for medical care if they get sick or hurt. Employers may pay all or part of the cost for health insurance. Some companies also offer dental insurance. Dental insurance helps people pay for checkups and dental care.

Companies also may offer customer service representatives sick leave and paid time off. Sick leave pays for days of work employees miss because of illness.

Customer service representatives provide information over the phone and in person.

Paid time off is similar to sick leave. But employees do not have to be sick to use paid time off. Many employees use paid time off to take vacations. Companies also limit the amount of paid time off employees can use.

Customer service representatives often receive discounts on products or services their companies offer. For example, representatives at stores may pay less for products at stores where they work.

Outlook

The customer service industry is growing. Many new companies are formed each year. Most of these companies have customer service representatives. The customer service industry in the United States is expected to grow faster than average. The outlook for customer service representatives in Canada is fair. The number of customer service representative positions in Canada is expected to remain steady.

Customer service representatives keep a record of customers' information.

Chapter 5

Where the Job Can Lead

Customer service representatives have many opportunities to advance. They can advance into other positions in the customer service field. They also may move into other careers.

Customer service representatives can become lead representatives. Lead representatives oversee teams of representatives. Lead representatives may help representatives deal with customers who require special attention.

Lead representatives can become managers. Managers oversee all of a company's customer service representatives. They listen to

Customer service representatives can become managers.

representatives' calls. Managers sometimes help lead representatives deal with customers.

Customer service representatives may advance to other departments in the same company. For example, representatives may become salespeople. Salespeople sell companies' products and services to customers.

Related Careers

Many customer service representatives advance into related careers. Representatives who work at banks may become loan representatives. Loan representatives prepare loan applications. They make sure applications are completed correctly. They also contact applicants' banks and employers to make sure information is correct.

Customer service representatives who work for utility companies may become investigators. Investigators review customers' bills. For example, customers may call representatives if they believe they were charged too much. Investigators then review the customers' accounts. The investigators

Customer service representatives can become lead representatives.

explain all costs included on the customers' bills. Investigators fix customers' bills if they are not correct.

Customer service representatives learn a great deal by working with customers. They learn how to work with all types of people. This skill can be useful in many careers.

Words to Know

call center (KAWL SEN-tur)—an office where customer service representatives receive customers' calls

catalog (KAT-uh-log)—a book that shows items customers can buy from a company

lead representative (LEED rep-ri-ZEN-tuh-tiv)— a person who oversees a team of customer service representatives

script (SKRIPT)—written information that customer service representatives use as a guide while talking to customers; many representatives in call centers use scripts.

utility (yoo-TIL-uh-tee)—a basic service provided to a community; utilities include telephone, water, and electricity.

warranty (WOR-uhn-tee)—a contract that a manufacturer or store provides for a product; companies will fix or replace broken products if the products have a warranty.

workstation (wurk-STAY-shuhn)—an area where customer service representatives work; most workstations have a desk, computer, and telephone.

To Learn More

Anderson, Kristin and Ron Zemke. *Delivering Knock Your Socks Off Service*. New York: Amacom, 1998.

Ettinger, Blanche. *Opportunities in Customer Service Careers*. VGM Opportunities. Lincolnwood, Ill.: VGM Career Horizons, 1992.

Ramundo, Michael C. *Complete Book of Ready-to-Use Customer Service Scripts*. Paramus, N.J.: Prentice Hall, 1997.

Useful Addresses

Communication Workers of America
Department of Apprenticeships, Benefits,
  and Employment
501 3rd Street NW
Washington, DC 20001-2797

National Retail Federation
325 7th Street NW
Suite 1000
Washington, DC 20004

Internet Sites

Canada Job Futures
http://www.hrdc-drhc.gc.ca/JobFutures/

The Customer Service Network
http://www.customernet.com

National Retail Federation
http://www.nrf.com

Occupational Outlook Handbook
http://stats.bls.gov/oco/ocos133.htm

Index